IGNATIUS SPENCER

by
Fr Ben Lodge C.P.

*All booklets are published thanks to the
generous support of the members of the
Catholic Truth Society*

CATHOLIC TRUTH SOCIETY
PUBLISHERS TO THE HOLY SEE

2

CONTENTS

BEGINNINGS

Introduction

To be born into one of the wealthiest families in Britain, to be educated at Eton and Cambridge, to have family guests ranging from Admiral Lord Nelson, through Sir Walter Scott, to Sir Joshua Reynolds and Isambard Kingdom Brunel, and to be a relative of Sir Winston Churchill, and the future King of England, is hardly the background one would expect to produce a potential saint. And yet this was the background which formed and shaped the Honourable George Spencer, who became better known as Fr Ignatius of St Paul. His life was marked by an absolute commitment to prayer; a conviction that we are all called to be holy; and a belief in the need for all Christians to work for the fulfilment of the prayer of Jesus: "That they may all be one." This last belief led George Spencer to dedicate his life to the cause of Christian Unity, and so he is increasingly recognised as the first apostle for unity in Britain.

Sources

We know a great deal about his life from a number of sources. He began to write his autobiography during a period of convalescence in 1835, but unfortunately it only extends up to his Grand Tour of Europe in 1820. However, he also kept a Diary which began in 1817, and went right through to a few days before his death in 1864. Frustratingly the Diary was suspended from 1829, a short time before his conversion, until 1846, just before he became a Passionist priest. This seventeen year period which is omitted, covers the time of his conversion to the Catholic Church, his studying in Rome under Nicholas Wiseman, his ordination and appointment, first to Walsall, and then to West Bromwich, and his move as Spiritual Director to St. Mary's College, Oscott.

Another major source of information about his life is the many letters he wrote. Initially he relied on his father to frank his mail (this cost nothing for Members of Parliament); and following the introduction of the Penny Post in 1840, Spencer continued to write to people at all levels of society. He records that on one occasion, as he was free from preaching, he wrote seventy two letters in two days. Occasionally he would write these letters while waiting in railway stations for trains. The fourth source of information is the recollections of his family, his fellow Passionists, and the many people who recorded their memories of him shortly after his death and sent them to Fr Pius Devine, his contemporary, and first biographer.

The Diary and letters weave a tapestry in which the life of an English nobleman can be seen struggling to find and follow the will of God. This struggle takes him from his comfortable living on the family estate at Althorp, through the towns and countries of Europe, encountering both the rich and the powerful, and the hopelessly poor. But it also presents a picture of an inner struggle between a man and his God, this struggle was to lead Spencer to risk losing his family as he gave up membership of the Anglican church and became not just a papist, but a Roman priest.

Convinced of the error of the Protestant church, George Spencer made it his life's work to make good the error, by an honest and open dialogue which he hoped would lead to "unity in the truth", and by organising a series of campaigns to pray for the conversion of England. This was not done out of a simple pietism, nor without any thought - George thought long and hard how best to achieve his goal, and efficiently marshalled entire groups of Bishops in Europe to promote the cause, while at the same time, he pleaded with the Irish to join their prayers to pray for the conversion of their former enemy and oppressor.

Background

The American, French and Industrial Revolutions were to have a profound influence on nineteenth century England. Major changes in Church, State and Society are touched on in the Diary and letters, not as some

distant phenomenon, but as something that George
Spencer is intimately caught up in. A fundamental
change was taking place in English society; one strand
of that society which was to undergo major upheaval
was the Roman Catholic Church, especially after the
passing of the Catholic Emancipation Act of 1829. In
one way it was this which enabled the influx of the
victims of the Irish potato famine to be ministered to in
the following decade, and it was this movement which
was to shape the Catholic Church in England for more
than a century afterwards.

Early Life

George Spencer was born on 21st December 1799, in
Admiralty House, Whitehall; this was because his father
was First Lord of the Admiralty. Lord Spencer supported
William Pitt the Younger, and had succeeded Lord
Chatham as first Lord of the Admiralty. While holding
that post, his administration enjoyed a great reputation for
the historic naval victories of St. Vincent, Camperdown
and the Nile, and also for the humane and just way he
dealt with a naval mutiny. He was a proponent of Catholic
Emancipation in 1829, and brought up his family to be
socially responsible, God-fearing people. The Spencer
family owned Spencer House, on the side of Green Park,
and looking across to Buckingham Palace. Another
London home was Wimbledon Park, the present site of the

Lawn Tennis Association. George was the youngest son of eight children. His mother, Lady Lavinia Spencer, was the daughter of the first Earl Lucan; she was noted for her beauty, and several times sat for Sir Joshua Reynolds. Other visitors to Althorp included Thomas Gainsborough, David Garrick, Gibbons, Johnson and Sheridan.

Politics formed a large part of the life George was born into. His brother John Charles became Chancellor of the Exchequer in 1830 under Earl Grey, and it was said that it was due to "honest Lord Althorp" that the Reform bill of 1832 was carried through. Furthermore, it was claimed that he was the only Member of Parliament who could read and understand the Government's book-keeping!

George appears to have been privately baptised, but, according to the Wimbledon parish records, was received into the Church of England in June 1800. Shortly after this, he moved to Althorp, the family estate in Northamptonshire. One of his earliest recorded memories concerns his sixth birthday. He describes how his sister's Swiss governess explained to him about the existence of God: "My memory may deceive me, but I have a most clear recollection of the very room at Althorp where I sat with her while she declared to me, as a new piece of instruction, for which till then, I believe, I had not been judged old enough, and that there was an Almighty Being dwelling in heaven who had created me and all things, and whom I was bound to fear." Spencer appears puzzled that this information had been withheld: "Till then, I had not the least apprehension of anything beyond the sensible world around me. This declaration, made to me as it was with tender seriousness, was, I believe, accompanied with gracious expressions, which have never been, in all my errors and wanderings, obliterated. To what but the grace of God can I ascribe it, that my faith in the truth of God should have been preserved, while for so long a time I lived as I afterwards did, wholly without its influence?"

Character

George's family background was heavily military, and so he frequently uses such imagery to describe both his life and work. He was an Englishman and an aristocrat, a truly noble man who became a good European, at ease with princes and prelates, Emperors and Kings. But he was first and foremost a family man, and always tried to respect the wishes of his parents. There was nothing he enjoyed more than being with the family, whether it was out hunting, or on holidays, or gathering for the celebration of Christmas - always a major social event in the Spencer household. The love and security the family provided, the beauty and culture of its surroundings had a major influence on George. He was particularly close to his brothers Fritz and Bob, but his favourite sister was Georgina who's death in 1823 left a lasting scar.

He frequently condemned himself for his bouts of idleness (which in fact were more likely to be periods of shyness), and recognised that he had several flaws in his character. The dominant one, as far as he was concerned was that he was given to periods of "melancholia" or depression; this was especially true in his early years when he would try to avoid any form of social contact with others, but he in fact struggled with it all of his life.

In the Diary, which he described as a record of his follies and absurdities, George would reflect on his character at the end of each year and also on his birthday, and submit himself to acute self-analysis. With real insight he said "I think any time of life is happy if one knows the secret of making it so." So he learnt to express gratitude to God, for he was always aware that only one thing in life was worth striving for, and that was God.

Eton

On 18th May 1808 George entered Eton College along with an older brother Frederick (Fritz); the boys lived with their tutor Rev. Richard Godley, an evangelical clergyman. This led to George developing a fascination for long prayers and ascetical practices. The prevailing

climate in Eton was one of bullying, and both Spencers
suffered on account of this. However, they recognised that
Mr Godley did his best to protect them and keep them
separated from the rest of the college. George saw Mr
Godley to be a conscientious and deeply religious man,
and the young Spencer was always grateful for the
influence of Godley. While George found the strict regime
oppressive, life was not all bad. While at Eton he
developed what he subsequently described as a "mania" -
his passion for cricket. The very first extant letter from
George to his mother in 1811 states in French that Fritz,
his older brother, has a black-eye from playing cricket. In
subsequent years, while on family holidays in the Isle of
Wight, while at Cambridge University, and even as
spiritual director in Oscott College, he indulged his
passion for the game. During one summer Godley took
George to Chester to visit his sister. While there George
read a number of pious books, and came back to Althorp
with a prayer book which was not to the liking of his
parents. This was to mark the beginning of the end of his
four years with Mr Godley.

EDUCATION

In 1811 Fritz left Eton to embark on a naval career. With no distractions George spent more time with Mr Godley, absorbing his religious ideas and a dread of wickedness. George's parents were concerned that Godley was not sufficiently Anglican in his beliefs, and so George was moved into the College itself at Eton. This proved to be a tough time for George, as he was exposed to the brutal system of fagging. He recognised that he was accepted by his classmates at the cost of giving up his devotions; he later admitted to his lack of courage in making a stand when they went out pilfering walnuts, turnips, ducks and chickens. He felt he had no friends to share with, and his faith in God had been sorely tried, and he claimed that for two years he did not pray. In his Autobiography, reflecting on his own failure to pray, he describes how on one occasion in the dormitory in Eton he is suprised to see his chief tormentor pray, making George realise how he himself had fallen away from the life of prayer. In fact George must have had a reputation for being pious, for the bully tells him not to let his mouth gape as George watches the bully pray. Reflecting on this unhappy period of his life, George claimed that parents have a clear duty to teach their own children virtue and piety. Only when this has been firmly established should a child be placed in a school outside of the family.

Having been removed from the evangelical influence of Mr Godley and his family in 1812, it was not long before George left Eton and was placed under the care of a private tutor, Rev. Charles Blomfield, Rector of Dunton, Buckinghamshire. Blomfield was a talented man who went on to become Bishop of London. George stayed with Blomfield for two years, developing a love for study and knowledge, something he later claimed formed him into a reading man at Cambridge and "thus [I] was saved from much perversion."

Within the Blomfield house, prayers were said on a daily basis, and "a prominent part of our instruction was on matters of religion." At Easter 1816 George was Confirmed by Dr Howley, Anglican Bishop of London, and later Archbishop of Canterbury. He returned to the use of prayer manuals, and spent more time in self-examination.

His mother wanted George to have the attributes of a young gentleman and so encouraged him to take up both fencing and playing the guitar; on both counts she failed. However, George was getting more involved in the social life of the Spencers in both Althorp and Spencer House; inevitably this meant attending balls and meeting young women. According to the Diary, more than one young lady caught his attention, and it would appear that George found it difficult to talk to girls. Fortunately he had another older brother, Bob, to guide and give him advice.

University

In October 1817 George went to Cambridge and entered Trinity College. It is at this point that he begins to fill in his diary each day, listing who shared breakfast with him, what lectures he attended, who he played cards with, and how many hours he spent reading each day. From Cambridge he would go over to visit Mr Blomfield, and occasionally turned up at home to surprise his parents. During the summer months while still at Cambridge, he spent time swimming in the river and playing tennis. On returning home to Althorp he would join the regular hunting parties on the surrounding estates.

In letters to his father at this time, George tells of his studies and his social life, and also reveals that he sees his business transactions to be a burden which he is not very good at dealing with. Several times he had to get his family to advance money to pay off debts.

Generally George enjoyed himself at Cambridge. He wrote "I found myself now for the first time emerged from the condition of a boy. I was treated with respect and kindness by the tutors and fellows of the college; my company was always sought, and I was made much of by what was supposed to be the best - that is, the most well bred and fashionable set in the University. I had all the health and high spirits of my age, and I now enjoyed manly amusements, being set free from the cowardly feeling of inferiority which I had to oppress me at Eton." He records that he does not have any memory of saying prayers, and suspects he stopped praying when he left Mr. Blomfield.

Tea drinking formed a major part of the social life of the university, as did playing cards. George was introduced to tennis and declared it to be "the best exercise for College." However, repeated entries in the Diary make it clear that he applied himself to doing a vast amount of reading, sometimes for up to thirteen hours in one day.

At the end of his first academic year, he went to North Wales with two friends for a "reading holiday." Having employed a cook and a waiter they settled down to a routine of swimming, reading, shooting, writing letters, exploring, and visiting the local gentry. George recorded: "After dinner we again went on the coast to shoot, and I killed a large sea gull, the first I ever was able to conquer. One of his feathers I am now writing with."

Having obtained a first class degree, in July 1819 he received the honorary degree of MA from the Duke of Gloucester. Obtaining this was no great challenge for the son of a nobleman, as the major requirement was that he attended a set number of lectures and be able to do a little bit of translating of Greek and Latin; nevertheless he studied well. He proved to be an excellent student and acquired a fluency in French, Italian, Latin, Greek, and

Hebrew. He later acquired a working knowledge of German, and even taught himself the rudiments of Dutch.

As the youngest son, George was expected to become a clergyman, and had been informed of this when he was just eleven. His sister, Sarah, wrote at the time that George "could scarcely keep grave the whole day, after he had heard he was to be a clergyman." Accordingly, at Cambridge, he applied himself to attending some theology lectures, attending chapel regularly, and receiving the Sacrament. Interestingly, from an early date he recorded his criticism of various preachers, and the way the Sacrament was conducted.

The Continental Tour

To mark the end of his time at Cambridge, his parents decided to take George on the Continental Tour, and so in September 1819 they set off; this was to mark the beginning of his life-long passion for travel. The purpose of the thirteen month tour was not only to broaden George's education, but also to give his father the opportunity to indulge his passion for collecting books (his collection subsequently went to form a part of the John Rylands library in Manchester); it also meant that the family could visit Lady Georgina Quin, George's older sister who was living in Naples - at that time, a British naval base.

The tourists took three carriages with them across the English Channel. In the first were Lord and Lady Spencer; George and Dr Wilson, the family doctor were in the second; and the third was occupied by a man servant and two maids. In addition the family employed an Italian courier to ride ahead and prepare accommodation for both the people and the horses. On arriving in Calais George subsequently wrote in his Autobiography: "a day most interesting to me, as I then considered, because the first of my setting foot in a foreign land, but much more, I now must reckon, as being the first on which I trod Catholic ground and entered a Catholic church." In his Diary George recorded all the towns they passed through, and from time to time passed comment on his view of the local population. He was very impressed by the cathedral in Amiens, but commented it was not quite as good as York Minster. While in Paris they visited the Louvre, theatres and the opera; and in Fontainebleau they inspected several palaces. The evenings were spent writing letters, or playing whist. However, they were not the only people travelling. George recorded of Geneva "This place is so full of English, that we could not get any room in the town."

Dr Wilson and George went to La Scala in Milan, and while they enjoyed the music, the ballet was described as a pantomime. On visiting the cathedral in Milan George was very impressed by the building. He was fascinated by the Catholic liturgy and wrote: "There was a procession all round the building, with incense burning, and with the priests singing anthems all the time, and a quantity of other mummery, the sight of which might well have driven Calvin to the extremities which he went to in the contrary way. The whole service is always in Latin, so that the people may not reap over the smallest benefit from it." By the middle of November the group arrived in Rome: "My father, the Dr and I walked to St Peter's and saw it out and inside. It was most glorious; but its size for some reason or other disappoints me, as it does all strangers; it improves upon acquaintance I fancy. The deception arises from its perfect proportions they say." After inspecting the sites of Rome, including the Colyseum [sic] and Forum, they found themselves making repeat visits to inspect the Vatican. The family moved down to spend Christmas with their daughter in Naples.

George persuaded his parents to allow him to continue south to explore Sicily while they returned home. While looking into the crater of Mount Vesuvius with Dr Wilson, a volcanic eruption took place and they quickly moved away. A few moments later the place where they had been standing was covered with molten lava. George later recorded: "Here was an evident escape which, in a mind possessed with any religion at all, could not fail of awakening some serious reflections." It was at this time

that he began to become convinced that his life had been
marked out for some special purpose.

Despite journeying through Catholic countries like
France, Italy, Sicily, and Austria George does not appear
to have been influenced by any religious sights. He
subsequently commented that he had not been brought up
with any anti-Catholic feelings, "but though I knew
nothing of what it was [i.e. Catholicism], I rested in the
conviction that it was full of superstition and in fact, as
good as no religion at all." His escape on Vesuvius
certainly caused him to take stock of his life.

The tour continued back up through Europe until they
reached Vienna, where the news reached them that his
brother Bob had been killed. Plans were changed and
they headed back to Calais where, in the library, they
found the news was unfounded. In his Autobiography,
George wrote: "I remember going on my knees in the
news-room, when I found myself alone, which I believe
was the first occasion for a long, long time I had made a
prayer of any sort, or gone on my knees, except in church
at service time. This I never gave up entirely, and during
this time I never gave up receiving the Sacrament;
explicitly I did not intend to commit acts of hypocrisy,
but must have gone on through custom, and a certain
sense of propriety, without considering that I was
mocking God." From Calais they returned to London to
celebrate the good news with the rest of the family.

ANGLICAN ORDERS

Another Tour

Having discovered his love for travelling, and starting to contemplate going to Greece, Spain, Egypt and Russia, George used the excuse of his brother's reported death, to go and tell his sister Georgina that the report was false. He was delighted when his parents allowed him to go to Lausanne by himself. In the Autobiography George states that he realised this would be his last chance of travel "for mere travelling's sake", for he would have to settle down to the role of a serious country parson. In a similar vein he recorded "I conceived that after this journey I should give up all thoughts of worldly vices. I was likely to be fixed at home till the time of my ordination, and should assume something of the character of a candidate for Holy Orders."

The Opera

On the way through Paris he saw Mozart's "Don Giovanni", and was so impressed that he saw it again on his return journey in November 1820. The opera tells the story of a seducer and blasphemer, who attracts the wrath of men and God through his arrogant disregard for their conventions. Later he wrote: "In short I felt as if it was almost my last occasion, and I was entertaining, alas! some wicked devices in my mind when I went to see this most dangerous and fascinating opera, which is in itself, by the subjects its represents, one of the most calculated to beguile a weak soul to its destruction. The last scene represents Don Giovanni, the hero of the piece, seized in the midst of his licentious career by a troop of devils, and hurried off to Hell. As I saw this scene I was terrified at my own state. I knew that God, who knew what was within me, must look on me as one in the same class with such as Don Giovanni, and for once this holy fear of God's judgement saved me. This holy warning I was to find at an opera house in Paris."

This experience proved to be a sort of conversion, and so he began to concentrate on his spiritual career. As the youngest son of an aristocratic family, it was natural for George to enter the Church; given the family background it would probably lead to his eventually becoming a Bishop. His mother had discussed with him her idea of his living in a new parsonage at Brington on the Althorp estate - a living that was in the gift of his father. At best it could be said that George's preparation for priesthood was leisurely. He employed a Jewish scholar to teach him Hebrew, and continued his study of Greek and Latin; in between reading books and sermons he would spend his time out shooting or playing cards. However, from time to time he would renounce these pastimes as he felt it was not the correct image he wished to convey. On 22nd December 1822, the day after his 23rd birthday, George was ordained deacon by Dr Herbert Marsh, the Bishop of Peterborough. On Christmas day he commenced his duties as a Deacon at Brington. On the last day of the year, he wrote in his Diary: "The year is now nearly ended. Shall I ever see the end of another? If not, God's will be done. I at least have enjoyed a plentiful share of his mercies for the time past. May he pardon all my sins and follies of the last year, and take me under his almighty wing, to conduct me in safety and virtue to the end of another."

As a Deacon, George was expected to conduct the Sunday school, and this he did with enthusiasm. At the same time as being Deacon, he also qualified as a magistrate and worked in Northampton court; he reported that on one occasion he had to commit a parishioner to gaol as a vagabond. On a pastoral level he prepared a large group of children for Confirmation.

Parish Priest

In June 1824 George received "Priest's orders" at Peterborough cathedral. At the beginning of the following year Mr Vigoureux, the Rector of Brington, resigned his living, and George was presented by his father with the living of Brington and became rector of the parish. From the beginning, George's pastoral commitment was evident to everyone. Day after day he went visiting through the villages and hamlets which made up his parish; he estimated he was responsible for 800 souls. He was constantly visiting the sick and the poor, and was seen to give away food, money and clothing - much to the alarm of his housekeeper. He was also able to care for the sick and the injured - on one occasion setting the broken leg of a man who had been crushed by a cart. Any spare time was spent preparing sermons which he often preached from memory. In his Diary George records that he frequently carried out the funeral rites for his parishioners, and often he reported having to bury several babies.

While living in his luxurious parsonage, built and decorated under the direction of his mother, he tried to live a simple and frugal life-style, thus enabling him to give more money and food away. His father tried to control this by cutting back on George's allowance. George responded by giving up wine and puddings! Furthermore he did all of his parish visiting on foot, so as to avoid the expense of a horse. At one point, but without telling his mother, he discussed with his housekeeper the possibility of turning the parsonage into a hospital!

George's encounters with people of different Christian traditions led him to try and talk with them so that they would see the error of their ways, but sometimes things did not always work out as he had planned. On one occasion he went into the house of an elderly Methodist lady, and after they had knelt down and prayed aloud separately, they sat and had a discussion as was their custom. The old lady said that she wished that somebody would tell her any of her faults. George said as mildly as possible, that she had one, a slight fly in the ointment. She asked what the fault was, and as gently as possible he said that she always contradicted people, "No I do not", she replied. "There you have done it again" said George. "No I have not" retorted the lady.

George's life took on a regular round of preparing sermons, visiting parishioners, going to the Infirmary, and calling in at the courts.

Questionings

Inevitably these social encounters, and his further reading, led George to question the tenets of his faith. Within the Anglican Church he moved from being High Church to Evangelical and Methodist, and even showed signs of Puritanism. The sure foundations George thought his faith was founded on, now appeared to be not so sure.

For several years George struggled with his doubts as he came to realise that all his theological knowledge was based solely on the Scriptures, and yet within the Thirty-nine Articles of the Church of England there were doctrines which did not appear in the Bible. He could not see how the teaching on the Holy Trinity could be learned from the Bible. He struggled with his inability to give consent to the Athanasian Creed which began "Whosoever will be saved, before all things it is necessary that he hold the Catholic Faith. Which Faith except every one do keep whole and undefiled, without doubt shall perish everlastingly." George gradually began to suspect that there was a major flaw with the Anglican Church.

The first light began to dawn while George was on holiday with the family in the Isle of Wight. He was reading St John Chrysostom's sermons on the true presence of Jesus in the Eucharist. Having finished Chrysostom, he moved on to St Gregory. Gradually he began to see the difference between Protestant thought and Catholic doctrine. George began to study more closely his understanding of Authority and Tradition, in a similar way to his contemporary John Henry Newman. Gradually George learned to change his narrow focus on the Bible to include the wider view of the Church, and so came to see that the Church must point to the person of Christ.

At this time the Diary shows George resorting to prayer more frequently, while at the same time he was examining his relationship with God. He also begins to show that when he encountered ministers of different traditions, he was prepared to talk to them about reconciliation and unity.

Catholic Contacts

In April 1827 George encountered his first Catholic priest Fr William Foley who was working around Northamptonshire. Foley proved to be a true friend and support, encouraging him to persevere with both his prayer and his studies. His Catholic contacts developed as he was introduced to Fr John Fletcher of Douai seminary who was chaplain to the Dowager Lady Throckmorton. Like Foley, Fletcher gave the same advice - a new experience for George who always received conflicting advice when he spoke with any of his fellow clergymen.

A crucial development began in November 1827 when he received the first of three long letters from Lille; they were anonymous, but years later he found out they were from a Miss Dolling, an Anglican convert who subsequently entered the Sacred Heart novitiate in Paris where she died. How she had heard of George's struggle with his faith has remained a mystery. In her letters she explains that she has heard of his struggles and says she has gone through a similar struggle, and concludes that George should examine the Roman Catholic position. She argued that Scripture without Tradition cannot lead to salvation; that it is impossible for people to understand the composition, inspiration and interpretation of the Scriptures without that Tradition; that it is only through an unbroken succession of pastors that the Tradition can

have been preserved, so only those pastors - the popes -
can tell people with any authority what the Tradition
comprises; that the creeds, liturgy, sacraments and
jurisdiction of the Catholic Church are therefore the true
Tradition of the teaching of Christ. In total the thirty-two
pages of the closely argued letters made George's
conversion inevitable.

Ambrose Phillipps

In the autumn of 1829 George had his first meeting with
Ambrose Phillipps de Lisle, a twenty-one year old boy,
who at the age of sixteen converted to Catholicism.
George was enormously impressed by Phillipps, and
while he recognised him as a poet and a romantic, he also
saw that Ambrose had a very sharp mind. This clarity of
thought was revealed in Garendon Park, Phillipps' family
home, when both George and the Bishop of Lichfield
were present, and there was a religious debate which
Ambrose clearly won.

The Catholic Emancipation Act was passed in 1829,
thereby removing obstacles to Catholics holding state
office. Phillipps used this new freedom to develop
Catholicism in England. In particular he supported the
work of Augustus Pugin, the Oxford Movement, and he
was instrumental in bringing the Cistercians to Mount St
Bernard Abbey in Leicestershire.

Phillipps, who despite his youth, gradually emerged as
George's mentor, introduced him to Fr Charles Caestryck
a Flemish Dominican based in Leicester. This wise priest
led George through a process of seeing that it was the
work of the whole Church, not of any one individual, to
interpret Scripture. Thus a unified and consistent
understanding would be obtained. Caestryck pointed out
that it was not only through the Scriptures, but by the
writings of the Fathers of the Church, and the insights of
the faithful, that Tradition developed.

BECOMING A CATHOLIC

Conversion

Towards the end of January 1830 George left Brington to stay for a week at Garendon Park, with Ambrose Phillipps and several other Anglican and Catholic personalities. On January 28th. he had his last conference with Fr Caestryck at Holy Cross church in Leicester. By the following Sunday, George was received into the Catholic Church, and immediately wanted to go back to his flock in Brington and tell them of the errors of their ways! Moving George to Rome as quickly as possible appeared to be a prudent course of action. Lord Spencer consulted Bishop Walsh, the Roman Catholic vicar apostolic of the Midland District, and they agreed to send him to the "Venerabile", or the English College in Rome.

The family in Althorp were shocked when they heard the news; George himself had been worried that the news would kill his father. However, Lord Spencer did not ostracise his son, but gave him an allowance, although considerably less than the £3,000 per annum he received at Brington. This was given unconditionally until his father died, when his brother Jack became Earl and forbade George from speaking to anyone while visiting

Althorp who was not of the same social class as the Spencers. Jack wanted to prevent his brother from converting the tenants.

His conversion was not easily accepted even outside his family circle. George often told the following story: "I was once attacked by a staunch Church of England man, who had been an old sailor, and who had lost his arm in the service, for what he thought was unworthy of my character and family, leaving my colours and changing sides. I answered him thus: 'Suppose you, my friend, had entered a ship bearing the King of England's flag, and gone out and fought many a battle against French cruisers, but then found out by chance that the captain of the ship was an outlawed pirate, who had no right to the colours which he wore, and was making you fight for himself, not for your king, would you let me call you a deserter if the next time you came within hail of a true king's ship you jumped overboard and swam to her?' The good sailor seemed to understand me, and said no more about leaving my colours."

Student Life

In March George left England for the English College in Rome. The Rector was Dr Nicholas Wiseman, three years younger than George, and an oriental scholar; the two men became good friends. Despite the friendship, this did not prevent George from criticising Wiseman, and he urged him to "apply his mind to something more practical than Syrian manuscripts or treatises on geology, and instead take up the English mission." Ten years later Wiseman became the President of Oscott College, and when the English Hierarchy was restored in 1850, he became the first Archbishop of Westminster.

Within a few weeks of his arrival, George met the Passionist Fr (now Blessed) Dominic Barberi. Dominic had been asked to help Sir Harry Trelawney, a recent convert in his seventies, to learn to celebrate Mass. George was to act as the translator, and with Phillipps accompanied Sir Harry to the Passionist mother-house of SS John and Paul, where Dominic was the professor of moral theology. Highly intelligent, Dominic went on to become a professor of both philosophy and theology.

For many years Dominic had longed to work in England, and repeatedly obstacles were put in his way; any opportunity to have contact with the English mission was seen as a real boon, hence his enthusiasm to help the recent convert. Dominic's longing to work in England was part of a Passionist tradition started by its Founder, St Paul of the Cross (1691-1775). Paul had always longed for the conversion of England and dreamed of sending Passionists not only there, but to the surrounding countries. Dominic was to fulfil that vision when he arrived in Dover on Guy Fawkes day in 1840, and set about establishing the first Passionist community in Britain.

The Passionists had been established by Paul of the Cross to preach the message of a God of love, revealed in the Passion and death of Jesus. The Rule of the Order was very strict and severe, with a great emphasis on poverty. The way of life for a Passionist was clearly laid down as one of being immersed in meditating on the Passion of Christ, and then spending no more than half of each year out on apostolic work preaching missions or giving retreats; the other half of the year was to be spent in prayer at the foot of the cross. The purpose of this was not only to draw closer to Christ, but to be able to serve all in society, especially the poorest of the poor.

The religious landscape in England was beginning to change. The Industrial Revolution had marked a huge population shift away from the land to the industrial centres and the navigation canals, which attracted many Irish Catholics. It was no longer legal to persecute Catholics, and in fact Anglican theologians in Oxford and Cambridge were beginning to turn a very critical eye on their own church, partly stimulated by the followers of John Wesley. This was to give rise to the Oxford Movement, which in its turn led to several celebrated conversions, not least of which was John Henry Newman. However, it is important to realise that this entailed only a handful of converts when compared to what was happening in the industrial centres.

Between Phillipps and George Spencer, Wiseman was being convinced, along with Dominic Barberi, that England was on the brink of conversion to Catholicism. It is virtually impossible for us today, one hundred and sixty years later, and after two Vatican Councils, to imagine the situation as the Catholic Church in England emerged from being a penal church. Despite the difficulties these men faced, Wiseman went on to become Archbishop of Westminster; George would become a leading missionary and apostle of ecumenism, long before such a concept had been heard of; and Phillipps would anticipate the Second Vatican Council by encouraging greater involvement of the laity. Dominic Barberi received Newman into the Church at Littlemore in 1845.

As a Deacon, George preached his first sermon as a Catholic in January 1832. On 26th May, the feast of St Augustine of Canterbury, he was ordained in St Gregory's church on the Coelian Hill by Cardinal Zurla, the Vicar General of Pope Gregory XVII. It was from the same spot that St Gregory had sent St Augustine to work for the conversion of England. The following day, the feast of the Venerable Bede, George celebrated his first Mass. George was only too aware of the coincidences.

Three days later George left Rome for England, and called in on Fr Dominic, now the Rector of the Passionist community in Lucca. Once more they encouraged one another in their enthusiasm.

Parish Priest

George arrived at Plymouth at the end of July, and spent some time with his family on holiday in the Isle of Wight. The following month he was appointed by Bishop Walsh to be the assistant priest to Rev. Francis Martyn in Walsall, "where the parish was as large as a diocese."

Mainly with his own money George built the churches in West Bromwich and Dudley, and contributed to the church of the Holy Family, Sutton Coldfield. In November Bishop Walsh dedicated and opened the church of St Michael and All Angels in West Bromwich. George was appointed to take charge of the newly constituted mission. No doubt because of his celebrity status, he was taunted by youths, stoned and even spat upon.

His pastoral work in Brington with the landed gentry and his father's tenants was no preparation for the work waiting for him in the Black Country. Here the Industrial Revolution was beginning to drive the British Empire. The working conditions and poverty were appalling. Typhus, cholera and consumption were rife. In a letter to his father, George commented that his time hunting rabbits on the Althorp estate had been good training for hunting out the Catholics who lived in burrows tunnelled into the slag heaps around Tipton, Darlaston, Dudley and West Bromwich.

There was a dire shortage of priests, and at this time no Religious Sisters were working in the area. George had to

establish schools just to teach the basics of the Faith, and
that meant obtaining property often in the face of
opposition from those who were anti-Catholic. One
property had been a pork shop which George adapted, but
quickly it became apparent it was never going to be big
enough as the numbers steadily grew. By this stage, the
Irish were beginning to arrive in large numbers, attracted
by the prospect of work in the furnaces and factories.
Towards the end of 1833 Bishop Walsh Confirmed
seventy Anglican converts in West Bromwich.

Each day for George was a remarkable feat of
commitment and endurance, given that he was living on a
starvation diet for much of the time. He would rise early
and after meditation, reciting the Office, and celebrating
Mass, he would spend hours hearing Confessions. His
meagre breakfast finished, he would set off around his
district, visiting the sick and dying, hearing more
Confessions, and giving individual instruction to his
flock. Always on foot, except when illness forced him to
go by cart arranged by some of his "wealthier"
parishioners, George would distribute whatever food and
money he had with him. The result was that often he
would get home in the evening without having had so
much as a drink of water all day. The evenings were
spent giving instructions on the Faith, and again hearing
Confessions, often till midnight.

In August 1835 he had an attack of illness (probably consumption), and so went to convalesce at Hagley in the home of his sister, Sarah, Lady Lyttelton. It was while he was there that he wrote his Autobiography. He also entered into a newspaper controversy with a number of ministers, clearly stating his religious beliefs. Today we may be alarmed at such open controversy, but these were a popular part of newspapers, and so George came to establish a national reputation for his defence of Catholicism.

While he was being nursed back to health, he had to put off his plans for going to Ireland; the original purpose was to beg for funds for the church in Dudley, but this gradually developed into a proposal to preach all over Ireland for the conversion of England.

Having established his reputation as a preacher he was constantly in demand to attend the opening of new churches and preach; among these were St Mary's Derby and St Chad's in Manchester. He was delighted to be invited to preach the inauguration sermon at the opening of the Trappist church of Our Lady at Mount St Bernard - a foundation made possible by his friend Phillipps.

George was painfully aware of the shortage of priests; for him the obvious solution was the Religious Orders. He wrote to Dominic Barberi in an attempt to get the Passionists to take over Dudley, but he warned of the jealousy of some of the secular clergy.

In June 1838 he went to France with Phillipps' family, again for convalescence after another bout of consumption. George spent a fortnight in Paris and was introduced by Lord Clifford to the Archbishop of Paris. George made the proposal for "A Crusade of Prayers for the Conversion of England." With a number of friends he launched the Crusade, the essence of which was to engage in prayer for the conversion of England; he believed that this was possible through prayer alone. This was to mark the beginning of his life's work, his "mission". Initially the English Bishops supported the campaign. Details of the crusade began to spread throughout Europe, and as far as British Guyana, Jamaica and even Persia.

SECULAR PRIEST

In May 1839 George was moved from West Bromwich to St Mary's seminary, Oscott where he fulfilled the function of spiritual director and Dean for the next seven years. Not only did he have time for letter writing, he was able to travel to Ireland and the Continent, enlisting the help of Priests, Bishops, Religious Communities, and even the Pope himself. However, he also kept in close contact with the students, and not only would he correct them when necessary, but would also arrange games of cricket.

One of his students, Francis Amherst, went on to become the Bishop of Northampton. He later wrote: "When Fr Spencer was Superior at Oscott, I had the good fortune to be under him. He frequently visited me and several of my companions in our room, when he would talk with the greatest earnestness of the conversion of England, of the sanctification of the priesthood, and of the entire devotion which should characterise a priest. Sometimes his visits took place late at night after we were gone to bed when, if we were not asleep, he would sit upon a chair, table or the edge of the bed, and speak of his favourite themes for an hour."

For some time since his conversion George had struggled with the idea of living as a Religious under solemn vows, as he believed this would lead to the greater glory of God. Already in Rome his spiritual director, the Jesuit Fr Glover, praised Religious life, but said that George was too old to adapt to monastic life. Naturally the Bishop did not want to lose such an able priest, and so made an arrangement with George that he would take over the administration of George's finances. This was not as a vow of Poverty, but it was the nearest he could get to it. At the same time George began to develop the notion of lay people living under religious vows, and in Oscott he tried to convince the clergy to recite the liturgical prayer in common, and to form the lay staff into what today would be recognised as a Gospel-based lay community.

On a number of occasions he wrote an account of his conversion which he submitted to papers for publication. One account states: "I am a brother of Lord Spencer. I was once a clergyman of the Established Church. In the year 1830 I became a Catholic, and two years later a Catholic priest. My family and my countrymen generally must, of course, judge me to have been greatly mistaken in taking these steps; but I have never, I believe, been deliberately accused of dishonesty, or insincerity on account of them. As an honest Catholic, I am bound to believe, what I do believe, what is of infinite consequence, temporal and eternal, to the welfare of my countrymen as individuals, and as a nation, that they should return to the Catholic faith, and I have devoted my life to the object of leading them back to it."

In January 1840 George visited Newman at Oriel College, Oxford while he was still Anglican asking him to pray for unity. This was the first proposal for a union for prayer for unity, and it had as its specific aim the unity of Christians. At first sight this appeared to be a disaster as Newman refused to see him. Subsequently Newman wrote in his Apologia that he had been "very rude to that most zealous and charitable man." George used a military image to describe the meeting: "I sailed right down into the centre of the enemies' fleet, and my little ship has been terribly battered and mauled. But I made good my retreat with colours at the mast head, and I look forward one day to a glorious victory." Little did he know that five years later Fr Dominic would receive Newman into the Church.

Today we can take for granted the idea of Christian Unity, and specifically work for it each year in an Octave of Prayer, but things were very different in the days of George Spencer. His view was that Christ had founded the Catholic Church, and so unity could only be achieved by those who submitted to Rome. However, George was not looking for institutions to amalgamate, but for people to come together. He was convinced that unity could be attained by coming together in honest discussion, and so one of his driving motifs was "unity in the truth."

George hammered home again and again in his preaching, that it was by prayer and spiritual renewal, by conversion to Christ, that we shall ultimately attain union. Frequently he pointed out that it was Catholics who needed to undergo real conversion before they could expect Protestants to imitate them.

At the heart of the crusade, or Association as it became known, was the intention to pray for the conversion of England. George realised that the English by nature seemed more reluctant to get involved with such an Association. He also had a struggle trying to clarify whether the intention of the Association should be specifically for the conversion of England alone, or should include all Protestants and separated Christians all over the world - as well as lapsed Catholics. He finally settled on the latter.

Opposition

Dr Peter Baines, the Vicar Apostolic of the Western District, issued a Lenten Pastoral letter rejecting the idea of public prayers for England, and he went on to make severe complaints against the influence of "certain converts." The language was so extreme that he was summoned to Rome where he was reprimanded, but he continued with his opposition to the crusade.

Because of the Pastoral letter, George had to limit his activities. In a letter to Dominic Barberi he explained that

he had written articles which resulted in donations to help
establish the Passionists, and Dominic arrived in England
in October 1841. Along with a number of the Bishops,
George believed that he would see England converted in
his lifetime, and that there were two main ways to
achieve this: the crusade of prayer and the arrival of the
Religious Orders.

With Dominic's arrival, the intention had been for the
Passionists to take possession of Aston Hall, at Stone in
Staffordshire, and establish their Retreat there (Retreat is
the traditional name given to Passionist communities);
however, the resident priest was unwilling to leave, and
so Dominic was advised not to visit the place. After
three weeks of frustration Dominic returned to Belgium,
still no nearer to establishing a foundation. While the
visit to England was a failure in its primary purpose, it
taught him to be more realistic. He now realised that his
hopes for the mass conversion of England was shared by
no more than a handful. The real situation was far
different from what Phillipps and George Spencer had
led him to believe.

First Irish Tour

George set off on his first preaching tour of Ireland in
July 1842; this lasted six weeks and he describes
preaching in Dublin, Carlow, Wexford, Waterford,
Kilkenny, Cork, Limerick, Ennis, Birr, Loughrea,

Galway, Castlebar, Tuam, Longford, Mullingar and Navan. Famously George influenced Archbishop McHale of Tuam to support the crusade. The Archbishop was passionately anti-English, but he was so impressed by George that he subsequently preached in Gaelic the substance of Spencer's sermon.

From July until October 1844 George went with the Phillipps family to tour in France, Belgium and Germany. The period of convalescence was anything but restful. For three months George laboured at promoting the idea of the need for prayers for England. All he asked for was support for the cause, prayer, and one Hail Mary daily. His enthusiasm was contagious, and generally people responded positively. His method was to reason that Catholic and Protestant need never fear the truth, since all truth comes from God. Frequently he made the point that he himself was an Anglican convert, and so he spoke from personal experience. Ultimately he argued that Catholic and Protestant could pray together - but he recognised that this would mean each in their own way.

While in Louvain he made a retreat, and gave serious thought to becoming a Religious, but did nothing to develop the reality. Back in Oscott, throughout 1845, many reports were received of converts entering the Church through the Oxford Movement. Of particular interest to George were Newman, Ward, Oakeley and Faber, all of whom had visited Oscott.

Becoming a Religious

In August George made a retreat under the guidance of Fr Thomas Clarke S.J. During this retreat he made his decision to join the Passionists. This was not as simple as may appear as George was faced with a choice. He was very impressed by the Jesuits and their missionary tradition; he was familiar with the Rosminians through his friendship with Dr Luigi Gentili; and of course there was the old friendship with Fr Dominic and the Passionists.

On 21st December 1846, his forty-seventh birthday, he joined the Passionist community at Aston Hall, Stone, Staffordshire. George received the habit of the Congregation, and chose as his religious name Ignatius of St Paul. This was in accordance with the Passionist tradition of giving up one's Baptismal name as a sign of leaving behind one's family. He then began his novitiate.

Despite being a novice, shortage of priests meant that Ignatius would have to start pastoral work immediately. The victims of the Irish potato famine were now flooding into England. Caring for the sick Irish people in the workhouse at Stone, Fr Ignatius became very sick and developed a life-threatening fever; in fact he was allowed to make his religious profession provisionally because he was judged to be in danger of death. After two weeks he began to make a slow recovery. Finally on 6 January 1848 he made his profession in the hands of Fr Dominic.

Ignatius never did things by half, and so he immersed himself in the life of a Passionist; this meant daily and prolonged meditation on the Passion of Christ, and then taking the fruits of that prayer life out on apostolic work. Despite his noble background he was more than happy to identify with the poorest of the poor, and to undergo any sort of humiliation if it would lead people to a love of God.

Throughout the rest of 1848 Ignatius spent his time giving missions and begging for money to develop Passionist communities. He was delighted to get back to West Bromwich and preach his first mission there. Subsequently he went on begging missions to Lancashire, the Midlands and London.

In June, Fr Constantine, the Superior at Aston Hall died and Ignatius was appointed as his successor, he was also made the temporary novice master.

In September he went as the first Passionist to Ireland and preached the annual retreat for students and staff at St Patrick's College in Carlow. Through much of November he was on a preaching and begging tour in Ireland.

Much of 1849 was occupied with preaching missions: with Fr Dominic at Westminster Chapel, and later the two gave the first Passionist mission in Ireland at St Andrew's, Dublin.

In August Ignatius set out on tour to Belgium and the Netherlands, with three aims: to beg for prayers for the conversion of England; to find novices to join the expanding Congregation; to get money to support the Passionist communities. While on this tour he heard of the death of Fr Dominic, and discovered Dominic had appointed him to be his successor as Provincial (Superior of all the Passionist Religious in England and Belgium).

From his days at Cambridge, Ignatius had shown he was not the best of administrators, especially when it came to handling accounts. But he was ably supported by some capable Passionists and so oversaw the development of the young Province. First they established a house in Hampstead, where he was the rector of the Passionist community at The Hyde (Edgware Road), and then they moved to Highgate. At times his brethren complained at the way he left all the administration to them, and occasionally he was rebuked. However, he was always aware of the work these men did, and frequently acknowledged it with gratitude.

The S.V.P.

On a number of visits to Paris, Ignatius had come across a group of devout young Catholic men and was impressed by their attitude. In September 1842 a Monsieur Baudon, was visiting England, and he called in to see Spencer at Oscott. His purpose was to try and excite interest in the Society of St Vincent de Paul. So successful was he that Fr Spencer promised to write an account of the Society and its work in the Catholic Magazine. This was the first introduction of the S.V.P. to the Catholics of England and Wales.

The following year Ignatius wrote to M. Baudon to say that he had only received one letter about the article from a priest in Lancashire. This priest, whose name is unfortunately unknown, wrote that he wished to co-operate in the establishment of "so beautiful a work." Ignatius concluded his letter with a phrase which embodies the attitude of the Society to all its works, "We must depend on the good providence of God." On 29th January 1844 M. Pagliano, a London restaurant keeper and a recent convert to the Catholic Faith, succeeded in gathering thirteen Catholic men together in London, and the first English Conference of the Society of St Vincent de Paul was founded.

A PASSIONIST

The Roman Catholic Hierarchy was restored in 1850; nevertheless, Ignatius records in his Diary that while he was on his way to Ireland "a man gave me two blows on the head" in Liverpool.

Because of his aristocratic background, it was easy for Ignatius to gain access to the top echelons of society. That same year Ignatius went to 10 Downing Street and requested a meeting with the Prime Minister, Lord John Russell; this was granted on the understanding that anything the Prime Minister said was his own personal view, and not that of the Government. This was accepted, and reportedly both men enjoyed the intellectual and theological debate.

Further travels

Ignatius preached a mission at St. George's, Southwark with two fellow Passionists; unlike his Little Missions in Ireland, these would extend from two to three weeks. In addition to the regular Passionist work of preaching missions, he also struggled with administering the growing Province, in particular the new Retreat at Sutton, StHelens. Furthermore, because of his fluency in languages he had to travel to Belgium to act as translator when the Passionist General came on a visit.

Through September to the middle of November
Ignatius was travelling, preaching the Crusade and
begging in Ireland. He met the Irish Bishops at their
Synod in Thurles. Following a pattern Ignatius had
established in Europe, he got himself invited to the
synod, and made a speech to them about the crusade. He
would try and get them to promise to encourage their
priests to join the crusade, and to get the priests in their
turn to encourage the faithful.

At the top of each page in his Diary, Ignatius would
summarise which towns he had worked in, and how many
days he remained in each place. So for a page in
September he wrote: "Carlow College 2. Kilkenny 2.
Carrick on Suir 1. Clonmel 2. Tipperary 1. Cork 6. Birr 3.
Limerick 3. Dublin 1. Newry 1. Dundalk 1. Ardee 1.
Carrick Macross 2. Dundalk 3. Castle Blaney 1.
Monaghan 2. 5 weeks".

About this time, Monsignor Brown complained to
Monsignor Grant, the Rector of the English College in
Rome and the agent of the English Bishops, about the
public wearing of the Passionist habit by Spencer. It was
judged to be provocative and antagonistic. In early 1851
Ignatius was rebuked by *Propaganda Fide* (the Roman
Congregation responsible for England at the time), for
wearing the Passionist habit in public. Later, at the
meeting of the Province, it was agreed that the habit
would not be worn in public, apart from within churches,

and Ignatius appeared to be happy agreeing to this. This was just as well, for in June 1852 Ignatius wrote: "After breakfast saw the Queen's proclamation against processions and religious habits."

An appeal for prayers for England by the clergy and people of Ireland, drawn up by Ignatius, was added to the Lenten Pastoral letter of Dr Cullen, Archbishop of Armagh. It would appear that Bishops found it difficult to refuse a request from the missioner. In May he was mobbed and almost killed near Charterhouse Square, London, apparently by an infuriated rabble, as a sequel to his visit to certain Baptist and Methodist ministers. Two months were then spent in Belgium, Holland, and Germany begging for money and asking for prayers for England. Ignatius records that he spoke for the first time in German in front of three classes of children in a convent school. It is important to realise that he did not restrict himself to calling only on Catholics; whenever the opportunity presented, he would visit the non-Catholic clergy and engage in discussion with them.

Ignatius left England for Rome in September 1851, not to return until April 1852. During that time he had four meetings with Pius IX. He told the Pope "Rome conquered England once under Julius Caesar, by the material sword. Rome conquered England a second time, more gloriously, under St Gregory, by the Word of God. I am calling on Rome to undertake this conquest again, under Pius IX, when it will be a vastly more important one than heretofore, and by means more glorious and more divine." It is reported that the Pope said nothing after this, but smiled.

He tried to obtain ecclesiastical approval for approaching Protestants with the express proposal to pray for unity. This was eventually refused, and when he was told of the negative response he said "Thanks be to God." While in Rome Ignatius tried to visit as many Religious Communities as possible, once more to enlist their support. He did obtain a special letter of recommendation to the Bishops of Ireland from *Propaganda* Fide.

On his return journey he had audiences with Archduke Franz Karl, and the Emperor Franz Joseph I of Austria. Ignatius tried to visit as many convents as possible, convinced that these could enlist more convents to help. He also wanted the Sisters to persuade the people they worked with, the sick, the elderly, and the children, to unite their prayers to the cause. In a similar way he would call on priests, and even had a meeting with the papal nuncio in Vienna.

Arriving back in England, Ignatius was moved to Broadway, Worcestershire, where he was the novice master. Despite this, he still spent a lot of time away from the community. It is worth noting that despite the importance Ignatius attached to Poverty, he was very quick to make use of developments in transport. Thus he frequently used trains (although always travelling third class! except when a kind Irish guard moved him up to second class). Ignatius realised that the train saved hours of time which could be better spent on the apostolate.

In July 1852 there were civil disturbances in the Liverpool and Birkenhead area tied in to the elections. Ignatius was giving a retreat to some Sisters in Birkenhead, and the parish priest sent twenty men to protect the convent. When all had gone to bed, Ignatius buried the ciborium with the Blessed Sacrament in the green house for safety. As it happened, the night passed quietly and there was no trouble around the convent.

Ignatius set off to make a formal visitation of the Passionist community at Ere, in Belgium. One particular problem was that a new building had to be found for the expanding community. Once again he used the trip to urge people to pray for England, and consequently he was away for two months. He met the Bishops of Belgium and France and used their influence to develop the movement of prayer for England.

In May 1853 Ignatius was appointed to run the mission at Barnet by Cardinal Wiseman. This proved to be a relentless round of giving instructions, baptisms, hearing Confessions, visiting the workhouse and the asylum. All of this was done on foot, including one day when Ignatius walked thirty-three miles because he forgot to take money for the return train journey. But Barnet was only half of the story, for he was constantly working in central London preaching in parishes.

Ignatius was a driven man as far as his Crusade was concerned, and he was determined he would get the support of as many people as possible. Thus he arranged meetings with Lord Palmerston and Mr. Gladstone.

Little missions

The last four months of 1854 were spent in Ireland where he gave sermons and lectures on the conversion of England; he argued that through the sanctification of the Irish faithful, the English would be so impressed as to convert. He made two more month long visits that year to Ireland. Gradually he developed his own form of mission, so instead of taking the usual three weeks to do a Passionist mission, Ignatius would take three days. The normal format would be to arrive in a town and almost immediately start hearing Confessions; Mass would follow, and then there would be a period of instruction, followed by more Confessions. If it was possible Ignatius would call in on any convents to elicit promises of prayers for England from the Sisters. After lunch he would write letters before taking more time for Confessions. Evening lectures were normal, and then Confessions would often continue until midnight; twelve hours in the Confessional each day was not unusual - always pleading with the people for their own inner conversion.

A century later the Second Vatican Council said: "There is no genuine ecumenism without an inward conversion . . . Conversion of the heart, holiness of life, and prayers in private and in public, for the unity of Christians, must be considered the soul of the ecumenical movement, and may rightly be called ecumenism of the spirit" (*Unitatis Redintegratio*, CTS Do 351, nn.7,8).

Ignatius would never take a day off, but would travel straight on to his next parish, often keeping this up for several months at a time. On some of his tours he would keep count of the number of sermons he preached by way of promoting the crusade - it was not unusual for him to deliver eighty or ninety sermons. These would vary in content from telling about his own conversion, talking about the different sects in England, and showing how the Irish by their prayers could change the situation. Many of these sermons would last for an hour or more!

In Ireland Ignatius used a rather neat argument to encourage the people to pray for England. He would explain that Jesus had said we should pray for our enemies, and if we did, then certainly our prayers would be heard. He proposed that the Irish knew only too well that the English were their enemies because of the way they treated them, so if the Irish prayed for the English, God would listen, and the English would become Catholic, and so no longer be the enemy.

Ignatius was moved from The Hyde to Sutton, St Helens. Additional to his work as missioner and preacher Ignatius took on the role of spiritual director of the "Sisters of the Holy Family" or Cross and Passion Sisters as they became known.

Ignatius spent seven months in 1856 making his last tour of the continent, begging for the new foundation of Blessed Paul's Retreat, at Mount Argus, Dublin. One notable encounter he had was with Napoleon III. After explaining his wish to see England return to the Catholic Faith, Napoleon gave him one thousand francs towards his cause.

He continued preaching in Ireland through the following four years. During 1859 he wrote to *Propaganda Fide* a document on the situation in Ireland. He asked that the Holy See should express the desire that the Irish devote themselves to the conversion of England.

At this point in the Diary, Ignatius begins to list the subjects he preached on. Inevitably there was a very clear pattern based on the Passion, and it appears that he would preach on the Passion in the morning and on some Christian virtue in the evening. Among his morning sermons were talks on the Agony in the garden, Judas, Caiphas and Peter, the scourging at the pillar, the crowning with thorns, the Women of Jerusalem. Some of the evening sermons dealt with brotherly love, zeal for souls, the Imitation of Christ, humility, and often as not:

the sanctification of Ireland leading to the conversion of England. A variation on this would be to preach on the seven last words of Jesus uttered from the cross.

Of course Ignatius did not have free time just to work on his own sermons. As more Italian Passionists arrived to work in England, he had to spend time not only correcting their written sermons, but also trying to improve their pronunciation.

APOSTOLIC LIFE

Ignatius continued preaching his little missions in Ireland through 1860, but at the Provincial Chapter (a meeting of the priests to decide policy etc., for the next four years), he brought under discussion the theme of "the sanctification and perfection of the Irish people." The Chapter Fathers agreed with and supported Ignatius' prayers and work. Ireland was also seen by Ignatius as a rich seed bed for new members of the Passionist Congregation. Consequently he was always looking for postulants, or young men, to enter the Religious Life. He had a certain amount of success with this, but he also experienced many disappointments. The idea of someone making contact with a Religious Order one day and joining two or three days later may seem strange in our day - it was not so a hundred and fifty years ago.

One difficulty he had experienced over the years regarding the Association, was how to record membership. At one stage he was keen that each parish which got involved, would keep a register - this public record, he felt, would galvanise people to remain true to the cause. The suggestion had been made that people should swear an oath in front of the parish priest, and then have their names recorded, just as was happening with the

Temperance movement which renounced alcohol. This also appealed to his sense of recording statistics. On the other hand, there were times when he felt that the administration simply was not worth the effort.

Throughout his time in London, Ignatius was a frequent visitor to Spencer House, recording on one day that he was fed "mutton chops." On later visits to London he was a regular visitor to various members of his family. By all accounts he was welcomed and greeted warmly. No doubt he was seen as odd and eccentric, but one member of the family subsequently recalled that he was simply "a character." It has been claimed that he was shunned by his family following his conversion. The fact that Ignatius wrote every month to his father after his conversion, suggests that this was not the case.

Again an incident involving his sister has been misunderstood: Lady Sarah Lyttelton was the governess to the children of Queen Victoria, whom Ignatius had met when he was a Catholic priest and she was a princess living in Kensington Palace. On one occasion Ignatius was going to visit Sarah but she wrote back and said he was not to visit her at Windsor Castle - and the part of the quote which is omitted goes on to say he is always welcome to visit her in her own mews cottage when she is not at work. Part of the reason for this was that the royal family were very protective of their children, and would not allow them to be seen by the general public.

Twice Ignatius made unsuccessful attempts to meet with the Queen as part of his campaign to influence all heads of state.

In August 1862 Ignatius was appointed Superior in St Anne's Retreat, at Sutton in Lancashire. The following month he went to Dublin for the blessing of the new Retreat at Mount Argus. Sutton was an ideal base for him as it was on the main railway line between Manchester and Liverpool; it also provided him with easy access to the Irish ferry. Ignatius had extended his preaching tours up to nine months - this did not go down too well with his community in St. Helens. Clearly they had difficulties trying to reconcile the Passionist ideal of spending six months at home, and only six months out on the apostolate. Fr Joseph, his deputy in Sutton, was left with all the administration of the community, but he did try to keep Ignatius informed of requests for priests to give missions or retreats.

How Ignatius had any "spare time" is a mystery, and yet he was constantly working on books, either writing them, or translating them from Italian. He wrote a short life of Paul of the Cross, and was still writing to newspapers promoting the Catholic Faith.

From time to time things would go wrong on a mission, so for example, maybe a priest had forgotten to advertise that Ignatius would be coming (sometimes the priest may only have had a day or two's notice). On arriving and discovering nobody there for the first talk, Ignatius would get the priest to take him to the "evening schools" and talk to the people there. He certainly was never going to allow an idle hour when it came to his mission.

One interesting alliance that Ignatius formed in a tentative way was with Fr Theobald Matthew O.F.M. Cap., whose campaign against alcoholism had an enormous influence not only in Ireland, but also England, Scotland and America. Fr Matthew had told Spencer that he would get the people of Ireland to pray for England. When he did come to Manchester he preached to 80,000 people, and in Liverpool 50,000. Ignatius hoped that the movement for Christian unity would someday become a similar popular movement, because it was even more important for eternal and temporal well-being than a temperance movement.

The writing in the Diary, covering the last few years of his life became ever smaller. How Ignatius was able to see what he was writing is a puzzle given that strong magnification is necessary today to read it. To give some idea, there are some pages which contain details of thirty-nine weeks of preaching and travel. Each day is recorded, the subject matter of sermons and the time spent hearing Confessions is noted, and he also adds in the times of trains and ferries he caught.

Towards the end of August Ignatius preached the retreat at St Clare's Abbey, Darlington. From there he went to Scotland and continued with his little missions, preaching his last one at St Patrick's, Coatbridge.

At 64 years of age, Ignatius began to anticipate his life was drawing to a close. More than twenty years earlier he had expressed the wish to die like Jesus "in a ditch, unseen and unknown." He was to get his wish.

On 1st October 1864 Ignatius was on the train travelling to Leith, near Edinburgh. He left the train at Carstairs Junction at 10.35, and had an hour's spare time before the Edinburgh train would leave at 11.50. He walked up the lane to pay a surprise visit to his friend and godchild Mr Robert Monteith. Ignatius collapsed and died by the side of the lane, about a hundred yards from Monteith's house; he was so disfigured by the seizure that when Monteith saw him, he did not recognise him.

Fr Ignatius was taken back to St Anne's, Sutton and was buried beside Fr Dominic and Mother Mary Joseph, in what has become known locally as, "the shrine of the three saints."

Health

Reading through the Diary one can be given the impression of an almost super human being, who had unbounded reserves of strength. When the body of Ignatius was exhumed, prior to it being placed in the new shrine, it was discovered that he had *spinabifida occulta*. This does not mean he had an open wound on his back, and it is possible he was not even aware of it. However, the considered opinion is that this would have made prolonged periods of walking quite painful; remember that while he was in Barnet he would frequently walk more than twenty miles in a day.

Ignatius, writing home from Cambridge as a student, mentions to his father that he suffered some bother with his teeth, and so was going to have to see the local dentist to "have his teeth plumbed." As a student, particularly on the Grand Tour, he suffered some problems with his eyes and so was regularly applying leeches to the area around the eye, this continued even while staying in Rome.

One illness which he never overcame was seasickness. Throughout his life Ignatius had a fear of travel by boat, and so was enormously relieved as steam boats proved to be more reliable and dramatically reduced the time spent at sea. From his time in Rome, through his priestly ministry in West Bromwich, and on through into the novitiate, Ignatius suffered from bouts of consumption or tuberculosis. For many this proved to be fatal, but even if one recovered, it left a permanent scar and weakness on the lungs. It appears that Nicholas Wiseman developed the same illness in Rome, for later Ignatius writes to the Cardinal about "our old complaint."As Ignatius got older and spent himself in a relentless round of missionary activity, he suffered various signs of ageing. He learned to recognise rheumatism as it took hold of his body, but he never allowed it to stop his work. On several occasions he ended up in bed as a result of severe "palpitations", and certainly there were times when he thought he was about to face death due to the severity of these attacks. He also suffered from a number of ruptures - the pain was so severe that it stopped him preaching on the conversion of England!

Sisters of the Holy Family

With the arrival of the Passionists, the Rosminians and the Redemptorists, there was renewed interest in Religious Life. This led to the founding of a number of Orders for women, including the "Sisters of the Holy Family", an Order founded by Mother Mary Joseph Prout. She had worked with a colleague of Ignatius, Fr Gaudentius Rossi, to establish an Order for working girls in the mill towns of Lancashire and Yorkshire. Their apostolic work was to provide education for the poorest of children, giving them a basic education and instruction in household tasks. It would appear that Gaudentius was not that well suited to helping to produce a Rule for women, and possibly he realised this. So when he moved to America in 1855, four years after the founding of the Order, he handed over to Ignatius the role of Spiritual Director. Among the tasks to be completed, was to present to Rome a Rule for approval - a Rule Ignatius was instrumental in re-writing. In May 1860 he received approval of the Rule for the Sisters of the Holy Family while he was in Rome at a General Chapter.

Ignatius saw Mother Mary Joseph Prout, the foundress of the Sisters, die on 11th January 1864, and she now lies buried beside Dominic Barberi and Ignatius Spencer. The Sisters subsequently changed their name to the "Sisters of the Cross and Passion."

As an interesting postscript, Fr Gaudentius in 1860, invited Ignatius to go to America, not to beg, but to stay there and become the Superior of a new Passionist community. He also suggested that he could found a convent of Passionist Nuns (i.e. not the Sisters of the Holy Family, but a group of enclosed contemplative women who lived according to the Passionist Rule). However, the General in Rome intervened and prevented any such further travelling by Ignatius.

On hearing of the death of Ignatius, Fr Gaudentius wrote in a letter: "Misunderstandings and oppositions served to show forth the unconquerable patience, humility, and charity of our dear departed Saint. Fr Ignatius was a soul all on fire with divine love - like that of St Ignatius - for Ignatius is from the Latin word ignis: fire. Ignatius means fiery, or full of fire. This was the reason, or rather cause, why he could never rest, for real fire can never rest. Like our Divine Saviour who went everywhere at least in Palestine to kindle the fire in the hearts of men, so our venerable Father went everywhere to kindle the fire of divine love and zeal in the hearts of men of almost all European nations on behalf of, or rather for, the conversion of England."

THE MAN

A month after the death of Ignatius, Richard Sibthorpe, an Anglican convert clergyman who subsequently returned to the Anglican church, wrote "One anecdote of him [Ignatius] - and I was pretty well acquainted with him - will give you his true character. I was to preach for a charity at Leamington, the occasion was a special one. He was to join me to sing the High Mass. He sent a substitute. Why? Because a poor woman was dying in the Birmingham workhouse, and he felt it his duty to stay with her all night, and aid her through the passage to the next world. He preferred the obscure duty to the Èclat of public appearance, where many eyes would have been on him. He was a very humble, honest, sincere and devout man, not a man of great talents or learning." Sibthorpe goes on to recall Spencer's visit to Newman in Oxford and how he "told me at Bath that he came back from Oxford in a most wretched state of mind. It was like a combat between a bear and a mouse. But lo and behold! It ended in the mouse getting the better of the bear; William Palmer [one of the Oxford men] became a convert to the Church of Rome, instead of Mr Spencer coming back to the Church of England."

R. Jeffrey of West Bromwich, a convert of Ignatius, recorded his recollections. "He was persecuted, scandalised, and nobly overcame his enemies. I remember one morning when he was going his accustomed rounds to visit the poor and sick, he had to pass a boys school at Hill Top. They used to hoot after him low names, but seeing he did not take any notice, they came into the road and threw mud and stones at him. He took no notice. Then they took hold of his coat and ripped it up the back. He did not care but went on, was out all day as usual, through Oldbury, Tipton, Dudley, Hill Top and the rest."

Testimonies to the sanctity and powers of Ignatius poured into Passionist communities after his death. One of his converts, Charlotte Woodward, wrote: "At one house where he visited, a child was suffering from a bad mouth, so that it was quite distressing to be with it. He laid his finger upon the child's tongue and blessed it and said 'it shall be well', and in half an hour it ate some red currants, and was cured from that time. My Grandmother to all appearances was at the point of death, there was the death rattle in her throat, and every sign of death about her. We sent for him, and he had no sooner touched her and spoke to her, than it ceased and in a few days she was quite recovered."

Charlotte continued: "He has been found in the gallery of the church [in Oscott] at midnight, after when a search had been made for him, lying prostrate in prayer. . . And he even asked my father to pray that he might become so poor that he would be compelled to lie down and die in a ditch. He always said 'We must go on, rejoice and thank God, it will all come right in the end'."

Throughout his life Ignatius was totally convinced that he lived under the constant protection of God. Once he spoke about the dangers during his walking from London to The Hyde. In wintertime a many great murders were committed on that road. Nevertheless, Ignatius preferred walking instead of using a cab: "I considered the matter and could not see why I should return home in a cab and incur that expense as long as I was able to walk. For God had care of me walking as well as in a cab. Therefore nothing could be in safer keeping than I was."

Gratitude to God was a keynote of the spirituality of Ignatius. From his time at Cambridge onwards, he thanked God for everything that happened: for sorrow and joy, sickness and health, contradiction and affirmation.

While still an Anglican priest, Ignatius wrote in his Diary: "I am convinced more and more that God intends me to suffer great things for him, and I ardently desire it." The suffering he so ardently desired was to become the hallmark of his later life, particularly as a Passionist.

The life of Ignatius was deeply rooted in the Passion of Christ, as is evident in his devotion to the Mass and his patience in suffering, whether physical, emotional or spiritual. His life's work from 1838 onwards, was the conversion of England; pursuing this cause, he met with insults, incomprehension, ridicule and rejection, but unlike his time at Cambridge when he saw himself plagued by indecision, now Ignatius was single-minded and relentless in pursuing his goal.

For Ignatius, the Passion and death of Jesus are without doubt the foundation of his spirituality, of confidence in God, and peaceful acceptance of His divine will. On numerous occasions he seeks to explain that the crowning point of confidence in God, is to give thanks to him in all humility in every circumstance of life, which in turn brings about a deep peace of soul. He does not set forth an explicit theology of the mystery of the cross, but bearing with the sufferings and difficulties that each day brings is, for him, the true way which Christ laid down for his disciples, in inviting them to take up their cross and follow him.

As a Passionist, Ignatius rejoiced at the insults and mockery he had to endure, because in this way he resembled Our Lord in his Passion. The following letter refers to the insults Ignatius suffered in Liverpool in 1851, while on his way to Ireland, because he was wearing his habit: "The example of my Saviour above all teaches it to me. He might have avoided ridicule, and He suffered it; and will anyone, who reads the history of his Passion in the Gospels, tell me that I, a Passionist, ought not to rejoice at meeting with some insults, and mocking, and even blows from vulgar people and rabble, in the streets of London or Liverpool, for the sake of my holy habit, after what he suffered for me in the streets of Jerusalem?"

In his letters of spiritual direction Ignatius was constantly directing souls to suffer in union with the Crucified Christ. He taught that the crucifix shows us the love of God, a God on the cross who is Lord and Creator of all.

After his conversion and departure from Brington, malicious tongues spread rumours about Spencer's relationship with Mary Wykes, his servant. At this point she had not yet become a Catholic. Writing to her, Ignatius said that she should pray fervently to the Blessed Virgin who herself had suffered such calumnies after the conception of Jesus: "Remember the most blessed and most glorious Virgin Mary; of all creatures the most beloved and most worthy to be loved of God, who was saluted by an angel as being full of grace and is now in heaven, queen of angels and prophets and Apostles and Martyrs. How her infinite honour of being Mother of God, was made the occasion of most cruel suspicions against her heavenly purity."

In a later letter to Mary Wykes he wrote: "Many wonders have been wrought by the receiving of the Lord in the Eucharist. Many by the intercessions of the Saints, but above all, of the Mother of God whom the Church teaches you to love and trust in, as your Mother likewise. Pray to God to give you a tender devotion to her whom he loves above all creatures, and who of all mere creatures is the most pure and amiable and exalted."In a letter to his cousin during his novitiate, Ignatius wrote of his trust in the Blessed Virgin, who had saved his life during an illness that was considered to be so mortal that Fr Dominic had indicated where Ignatius should be buried: "Oh! If my heart would throw off its binding and become free and ductile. . . I hope I shall begin indeed to love Our Blessed Lady and Mother, to whom I was commended, and who, I am persuaded, delivered me."

As we have seen, Ignatius was not always the best of administrators, nor was he always practical in some of his proposals. However, it must be acknowledged that sometimes an idea may be formed long before the words are created which are capable of expressing that idea. He produced a paper, in which he proposed the living of the Evangelical Counsels (the vows of Poverty, Chastity and Obedience, taken by members of Religious Orders), and the sharing of goods in common, **but for lay people.** Unfortunately the paper has been lost, but it was circulated on the continent and obtained limited acceptance among some of the bishops until Fr Ignatius received an order from his Superior General to "stop talking of the counsels etc." This was a keen disappointment to Ignatius, but his reaction was typical, he simply said "*Deo gratias.*"

Ignatius was convinced that the sanctification of the Irish people was intimately linked with the conversion of England. A fervently virtuous Catholic Ireland, forgiving and charitable towards England - a country they regarded as the oppressor - and Ireland praying for England's conversion, would, he argued, be powerful in its intercession before God. Ignatius lived and preached the Passion of Christ so effectively among the suffering Irish that their devotion to the Mass and the Stations of the Cross, and their patient acceptance of suffering as being a sharing in the Passion, became permanent characteristics of the spirituality of Ireland.

The ability to communicate came naturally to Ignatius. In addition to his Diary, he constantly wrote letters to his friends, religious superiors, and to those who sought him out for spiritual direction. He spent a number of years translating books from the Italian, including a short life of St Paul of the Cross, and a two volume work on "Thoughts and Reflections on the Passion of Christ." In addition to writing various accounts of his conversion, he wrote numerous articles for newspapers defending the Catholic Faith. Often his sermons would be published in papers, sometimes at the insistence of the local bishop.

Hallmarks of the Spirituality of Ignatius

No person could have lived the life Ignatius did without having a strong inner life. His life of prayer is solid and established in sound liturgy and doctrine. Writing to his Provincial on one occasion, he famously thanks God that he is not given to visions!

In his letters of spiritual direction Ignatius repeatedly insists that humility is the first necessity if there is to be any growth in a life of prayer. He argues that the principle is based on Jesus saying that we must become like little children, for "God teaches his true children to see wisdom and beauty in what others fancy to be foolishness." Ignatius claims that a person who lives a life steeped in humility will be ensured perfect peace of mind, for they will know that they are following God's will, and God will take care of everything. However, humility does not just "happen", it is something which must be prayed for; without it there is no foundation for the other virtues to be built on.

Solid peace of heart, Ignatius teaches, is possible only when one conforms to the will of God. This teaching emerged from his own experience of illness, and also from constantly seeing the hand of God in his life. Knowing that God was always present in his life enabled Ignatius to act boldly, in marked contrast to his often hesitant nature. He recognised that submitting oneself to the will of God, and sacrificing one's own will, was always a pleasing gift to God. This was not to be seen as some sort of negative action, but rather a very positive one, preparing us for union with God.

Ignatius believed that indifference to temporal things, and a willingness to accept sacrifices, are the sure road to conforming one's own will to the will of God. Union with the will of God prepares us for eternity, and so the best we can do is to entrust ourselves totally into the hands of God.

Despite his tendency towards "melancholia", Ignatius learned to live according to a principle of never being sad - apart from sorrow for his own sins and those of others. He said that he had learned to rejoice in all the troubles of life, because he knew that they formed a part of God's will, and so there must be a purpose in them. A state of perpetual sunshine in our soul depends not on outward circumstances, but on inward virtue, and especially on our conformity with the will of God.

Thankfulness in all circumstances of life is a frequent theme in the writings of Ignatius. He states it is the result of complete submission to the will of God, which he always tries to do, and he encourages those whom he directs to do likewise. He reasons that it is better to give thanks to the Lord than to bemoan one's lot. To become a thankful person is one way to overcome being a person who constantly moans.

Again and again he stressed the need to give thanks to God, no matter how severe the trials and sufferings. Even when one did not feel like praying, because of apathy and indifference we must still thank God. Ignatius

quotes Paul of the Cross to show that in sickness we
must thank God: "Blessed Fr Paul used to say that a long
sickness was one of the greatest of God's mercies, and I
am sure it is better when we are afflicted with sickness,
or with any other trouble sent us by Providence, to
accept it with love and thankfulness, than with sorrow;
and rather than wishing it to pass by before God's own
time, to pray that he will not remove it, till it has
operated to the full extent, all the good which he designs
it for in his mercy. Let us thank and praise God for all
things, sweet and bitter, rough and smooth."

During his last retreat, to the Poor Clares at
Darlington, they recorded that "His discourses were very
practical and spiritual, and delivered in a simple familiar
manner, and he always expressed himself with the
greatest humility, and was most condescending and
anxious to satisfy each one in private. He impressed
particularly the community of thanking God for all,
especially troubles."

One compelling idea Ignatius tried to develop over the
years was that of the sanctification of the laity. Writing an
account of this to his Provincial he explained he had: ". . .
thoughts, which I have had in my mind for many years,
ever since I became a Catholic, of the way to lead persons
to perfection in greater numbers, by the observance of the
evangelical counsels, by many who cannot or are not
disposed to enter any religious order. This was the

thought I was proposing for myself for sixteen years, before I found it was my vocation to become a Passionist ...At last when I became a Passionist, which I have never had a doubt was truly God's call to me, I passed some years without attending to my former plans, though I had never seen them to be false in principle."

He goes on to argue that such a group of lay people, striving for perfection in their own lives, would be of enormous help in the active apostolate. Furthermore, he states that when other people would see this group living like the early Church, they could not fail to be influenced. Ignatius was convinced that if Protestants could see being lived out in practice, what they were being taught theoretically about primitive Christianity, then they could not help but return to the Catholic Faith.

The point is that Ignatius was a visionary in the true sense. He anticipated by a century and a half the Second Vatican Council's call to the laity to be more fully engaged in the life and apostolate of the Church. His bringing the S.V.P. to Britain; his trying to empower Religious Sisters to take on the role of evangelisers and catechists; and his attempt to create some sort of lay-community, all reveal him to be a most extraordinary man. A man on fire with zeal for the love of England, an England which would be returned one day to the Catholic Faith.

Conclusion

In 1973, as a first step in the process of the introduction of the Cause for Beatification, the mortal remains of Ignatius Spencer were exhumed from the old church of St Anne's, Sutton, and re-interred alongside the tombs of Blessed Dominic Barberi, and Mother Mary Joseph Prout, in the new church built in their honour.

The diocesan process for canonisation was set in motion in July 1992 by Archbishop Worlock of Liverpool.

The Passionists

The Passionist Congregation was founded in Italy in 1720 by St Paul of the Cross, and brought to England in 1841 by Blessed Dominic Barberi. It is a worldwide Order of priests and brothers who preach the love and suffering of the Crucified Christ.

Further information about Blessed Dominic Barberi, or Mother Mary Joseph Prout may be obtained from:

The Secretary,
Sutton Shrine Trust,
St. Anne and Blessed Dominic,
Monastery Lane,
Sutton,
St. Helens,
Merseyside.
WA9 4ZD

The Postulator

For further information about Fr Ignatius Spencer, and with information about favours received through his intercession, please contact the Vice-Postulator:

Fr Ben Lodge, C.P.,
The Retreat,
3 Sea Street,
Herne Bay,
Kent
CT6 8SP